W9-BTM-856

MTV
MUSIC TELEVISION®

BOOK NO.

03

OVERGROUND

First Published in the United States of America in 2005
by Universe Publishing

UNIVERSE PUBLISHING
A Division of Rizzoli International Publications, Inc.
300 Park Avenue South
New York, NY 10010
www.rizzoliusa.com

© 2005 MTV Networks. All Rights Reserved.

All rights reserved. No part of this publication may be reproduced,
stored in a retrieval system, or transmitted in any form or by any
means, electronic, mechanical, photocopying, or otherwise, without
prior consent of the publisher.

2005 / 10 9 8 7 6 5 4 3 2 1
Printed in China
Library of Congress Catalog Control number: 2005936328

ISBN-10: 0-7893-1390-1
ISBN-13: 978-0-7893-1390-4

NEW DESIGNS FROM THE ART TOY REVOLUTION

Universe

SERIES EDITOR: Jacob Hoye
ART DIRECTION: Gabriel Kuo|brm
PHOTO EDITOR: Walter Einenkel
EDITED BY: STRANGEco

INTRODUCTION

In the summer of 2001 I was handed a 6-inch vinyl toy created by Hong Kong artist Eric So. It featured a kid in muted blue (see top of p. 160), decked out in white and red sneakers, a puffy down jacket, backpack, and baseball cap. This little toy was all attitude, dressed in its fresh gear with an expression that was simultaneously playful and streetwise. I'd never seen anything like it before and wondered exactly what it was I was holding: a cool, arty little icon combining elements of action figures I loved as a kid with a grown-up sense of style. I wanted to see more.

This moment was my entry point into the pop-culture phenomenon of Art Toys. Also known as Urban Vinyl or Designer Toys, they emerged in the late '90s and exploded into worldwide recognition through an overlapping network of subcultures: urban art, street fashion, U.S. and Japanese toy collecting, alternative comics, music, and contemporary art and design. In just over five years and with the do-it-yourself philosophy of an independent music scene, an international community of artists and companies turned action-figure design into a means to create affordable 3D art. The results are equal parts beautiful, irreverent, creepy, aggressive, cute, hilarious . . . and always extraordinary to behold.

Art Toys trace their roots to Tokyo and Hong Kong. Beginning in the *Harajuku* district of Tokyo (an epicenter for youth culture and fashion), a small handful of streetwear clothing brands, including Bounty Hunter and A Bathing Ape, cre-ated original toys as promotional items for their growing apparel labels. Meanwhile, a group of toy collectors and shop owners in Hong Kong began holding semi-regular toy conventions to showcase their wares. Influenced by what was happening in Japan, artists Michael Lau and Eric So joined the convention by creating their own original toys, often reflecting Hong Kong's thriving urban youth culture. By 2001 the convention had officially evolved into the Hong Kong Toycon, an international event featuring more than a dozen new independent toy brands.

By early 2002 the rest of the world was taking notice and the fan base for Art Toys leapt across the Pacific. Retail shops dedicated to Art Toys have opened in virtually every major city. Art galleries have begun to feature toys in their exhibitions. Most amazingly, scores of artists from various subculture art genres—graffiti art, underground comics, skateboard graphics, illustration, contemporary "low brow" art—have taken the opportunity to transform their art into beautiful vinyl sculpture.

Rather than a history lesson, this book is a celebration of style, process, and design. More than 300 toys are featured, along with some of the art that inspired them as well as interviews with artists, producers, and impresarios who contribute to Art Toy culture. Are they toys, or are they art? Does there have to be a distinction? I invite you to have fun deciding for yourself.

Jim Crawford, STRANGEco

↓
ARTIST COUNTRY ORIGIN COLOR CODE

AUS ↙ ARG ↙ CAN ↙ FRA ↙ DEU ↙ HKG ↙ ITA ↙ JPN ↙ ESP ↙ UK ↙ USA ↙

←

BIGFOOT
Bigfoot One

`SPECS`
> produced by: STRANGEco/Fifty24SF
> origin: USA
> size: 13"

↓

`SEEN`

THE DAYS OF BABY BLOCKS ARE ON THEIR WAY OUT. THIS IS THE BEGINNING OF HOW WE WILL SEE TOYS IN THE FUTURE.

↑

METHOD JAM
Roy Miles, Jr.

`SPECS`
› produced by:
   Warning Label Design
› origin: USA
› size: 2.5"

↑

IMPERIAL ONE
Roy Miles, Jr.

`SPECS`
› produced by:
   Warning Label Design
› origin: USA
› size: 2.5"

↑

O`SHEA
Roy Miles, Jr.

`SPECS`
› produced by:
   Warning Label Design
› origin: USA
› size: 2.5"

↗

BITDZ: BACK IN THE DAYZ FIGURES
[opp top]
Roy Miles, Jr.

`SPECS`
› produced by:
   Warning Label Design
› origin: USA
› size: 2.5"

↗

SPANKY VINYL FIGURES
[opp mid]
Spanky

`SPECS`
› produced by: Headlock Studio
› origin: Japan
› size: 3"

→

MONSTER TEENS
[opp bot]
Charles Burns

`SPECS`
› produced by:
   Sony Creative (Japan)
› origin: USA
› size: 2.5"

STASH 100% + 400% KUBRICKS
Stash

SPECS
> produced by: Medicom Toys
> origin: USA
> size: 3" + 12"

THREE ZERO TROOPER
Three Zero

SPECS
> produced by: Three Zero
> origin: Hong Kong
> size: 12"

↘

IN-CROWD
James Jarvis

SPECS
> produced by: Amos Novelties
> origin: UK
> size: 4" each

JAMES JARVIS & RUSSELL WATERMAN

Amos Novelties

James: I first met Russell and his partner, Sophia, briefly in 1992 or 1993 when I went to show them my work as a very innocent young art student in Brighton.

Russell: I was working at Slam City Skates. James would come into the store and later we found out that he was an illustrator.

James: I moved back to London to do an MA at the Royal College of Art and went in to see them again. I drew some ads for the shop.

Russell: Paul Sunman (main man at Slam) commissioned him to do some ads for the store. Sofi (Silas & Maria's designer, also originally working at Slam) loved his stuff and commissioned him to do some illustrations for Holmes, the clothing brand we were working on at the time.

Friendships grew, and we used him more and more to do catalogues, etc. His style became very much linked with Holmes.

James: The ads I did for Slam were the first proper published work I did, and it did a lot to define the kind of work I got later on as a freelance illustrator. Being involved with the then newly trendy skate scene got me noticed by magazines like *The Face* and *i-D*, and by and by more mainstream jobs came along.

What are your individual backgrounds, and how did this possibly lead to the toy world?

James: I grew up in suburban South London, obsessed with drawing. I liked Richard Scarry, Hergé, and 2000 AD. All I wanted to do was draw. I went to college to study illustration. At college I decided I wanted to draw cartoon characters that weren't human, that were their own thing. I had an idea that they could be like Bauhaus cartoon characters, very minimal. Form follows function. They would have only the features they needed to be expressive. I was also into drawing car parks, as I wanted somewhere for these characters to live. From that came my concept of the potato-headed multiverse.

In 1997 it was suggested I could make one of the characters I drew for Holmes into a toy. I had no idea such a thing was possible. I made some technical drawings and sent them off. This toy ended up being Martin, the first figure I made with Silas & Maria.

In rationalizing the toys as part of my work I decided that they were simply another byproduct of drawing, like illustrations or comic strips or paintings. For me, drawing is the primal thing.

Russell: I come from a pretty anonymous background, having grown up in the suburbs of London. Always been into music and skating so once I left college a job with Rough Trade

Record Store/Slam City Skates seemed like the right thing to do. Needed cash as I already had a kid with my partner. Pretty much had more kids and worked hard at Slam. Got more into fashion/street culture and ended up involved with Slam City's importing branch and directing an in-house clothing brand. Eventually, I left with Sofi, and together we started Silas & Maria. We were bored with the way skating was going and how this was restricting what we could produce design-wise. A few years into Silas we then started Amos Novelties. I am a strong advocate of small independent businesses. Here lies the only path to the successful and true marrying of commerce with cultures. Amos had to be created to complement Silas.

The first toy we created was begun in 1997. The toy was released in 1998. At that time I think that Bathing Ape and Bounty Hunter (both fashion brands from Japan and both the real pioneers) had released their first figures. Medicom was also doing their thing, but at that time they were much more closely linked with the established toy collector market (this predates their creation of the Kubrick and Be@rbrick platform toys). We were a small clothing company producing a toy, and we were blown away by our ability to do this. Toys were for mass production! James was incredibly impressed that one of his illustrations had become a physical entity. We had never thought that it would be possible for a company with our resources to do this.

The two of you are generally credited as among the pioneers in limited-edition, boutique-style toys. How have you seen this all change in the eight years you have been creating toy designs?

James: I think that more people have realized that making a toy isn't an inaccessible industrial process. If you have a bit of money it is very easy to make a small-run toy.

Russell: There's too much of the stuff now. Too much crap. This is a bit of an outspoken view, but what the fuck, eh.

You both started with creating figures for Silas & Maria. What prompted the decision to spin Amos off as a separate company?

James: Silas is a fashion company. Toys aren't fashion. It seemed obvious to separate the two. Having made a set of toys with Sony, I realized that I wasn't happy with a big company buying into something that we had developed independently. So it made sense to do something on our own—we already had an audience through what we had achieved with Silas.

Russell: Originally the toys were a promotional tool for Silas, but they ended up taking on a life of their own. This is why we started Amos. To give James a full-time occupation and to give these figures the breathing space they required. We have always wanted to get these figures into a more mainstream market (but on our terms). Therefore we needed to get them away from fashion to allow them to develop to their full potential. This is how I went from having an interest in music and skateboards to co-owning a company that produces toys.

Where do you see this crazy toy thing going?

James: I think the reason our toys are good is because I think a lot about cartoon characters and spend my life drawing them. I think there is a depth to them, they can tell stories. I think this is what will keep them alive beyond the finite life of the limited-edition collectible market.

Russell: From our perspective, we would like to reach a wider audience. I would like to think that the better companies/designers in the new independent toy scene will do just that. Having an exclusive toy scene is a bit passé. Good work deserves to grow beyond a relatively small subculture. Other than that, I fear for the world's resources. Too much plastic/vinyl is being used. It's a petroleum byproduct. It will run out. We are planning ahead. We are talking about working with wood at present. We are also looking at a soya-based material with the strength and consistency of vinyl. I have heard of a cereal-based product too. Exciting times!

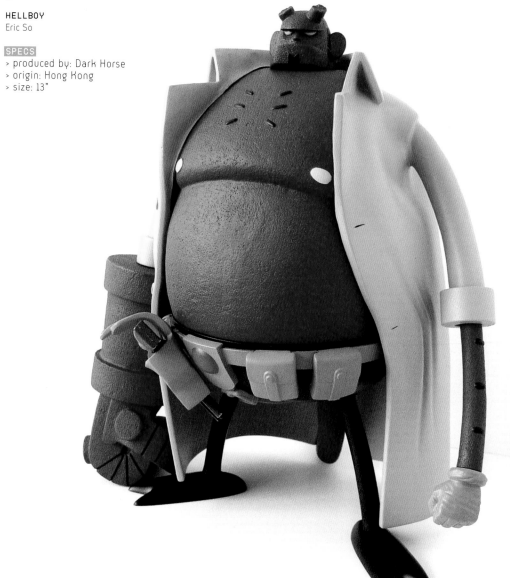

HELLBOY
Eric So

SPECS
> produced by: Dark Horse
> origin: Hong Kong
> size: 13"

↓

KEVIN MAK

TOYS ARE NO LONGER FOR CHILDREN ONLY. TOYS ARE NO LONGER SOMETHING JUST TO PLAY WITH. THEY BECOME A FORM OF EXPRESSION WE CAN NOW USE.

↓

GROUNDBREAKER
SEEN

SPECS
> hand-made custom
> origin: USA
> size: 12"

↓

SPRAYCAN MONSTER
SEEN

SPECS
> produced by: Toy Tokyo
> origin: USA
> size: 12"

↓

MS6
SEEN

SPECS
> hand-made custom
> origin: USA
> size: 12"

↓

KING
Tim Tsui

SPECS
> produced by: DaTeamBronx
> origin: Hong Kong
> size: 6"

↓ ↓

DAPE: KONG + PENNY
Tim Tsui

SPECS
> produced by: DaTeamBronx
> origin: Hong Kong
> size: 6" each

↑

**I.NSURGENTS W.ILDERNESS
G.RUPPO VINYL FIGURES**
Patrick Ma

`SPECS`
> produced by: Rocket World
> origin: USA
> size: 5"-7" each

↗

OCHO [opp top left]
Patrick Ma

`SPECS`
> produced by: Rocket World
> origin: USA
> size: 6"

→

HANNIBAL [opp bot left]
Patrick Ma

`SPECS`
> produced by: Rocket World
> origin: USA
> size: 7"

↗

ODYSSEUS [opp top right]
Patrick Ma

`SPECS`
> produced by: Rocket World
> origin: USA
> size: 7"

→

TITUS [opp bot right]
Patrick Ma

`SPECS`
> produced by: Rocket World
> origin: USA
> size: 7"

BOO

QTY:	1	PC
COLOR:		
N.W.:		
G.W.:	158	G
DIM.:	188	G
	135x115x120MM	

↗

BOO IN ORANGE
Touma

SPECS
> produced by: Wonderwall
> origin: Japan
> size: 5"

UGLY DOLL PLUSH
David Horvath and Sun-Min Kim

SPECS
> produced by: Pretty Ugly
> origin: USA
> size: 12"

UGLY DOLL VINYL
David Horvath and Sun-Min Kim

SPECS
> produced by: Critterbox
> origin: USA
> size: 7"

. . . HOVERING BETWEEN AN ART PRINT AND SCULPTURE BUT WITH THE PLAYFULNESS OF AN OLD-SCHOOL TOY.

↑
TREE DWELLER
Nathan Jurevicius

SPECS
> produced by: Flying Cat
> origin: Australia
> size: 7"

↑

NAAL
Nathan Jurevicius

SPECS
> produced by: Flying Cat
> origin: Australia
> size: 2.5"

↑

AARKSHI
Nathan Jurevicius

SPECS
> produced by: Flying Cat
> origin: Australia
> size: 2.5"

↑

BENNZI
Nathan Jurevicius

SPECS
> produced by: Flying Cat
> origin: Australia
> size: 2.5"

↖

MINI SCARYGIRL SERIES
Nathan Jurevicius

SPECS
> produced by: Flying Cat
> origin: Australia
> size: 3" each

↑

MINI TREEHOUSE
Nathan Jurevicius

SPECS
> produced by: Flying Cat
> origin: Australia
> size: 2.5" each

HONEYPOT
Toxic Teddies

SPECS
> produced by: Superfun Company
> origin: USA
> size: 3"

DED TEDDY
Toxic Teddies

SPECS
> produced by: Superfun Company
> origin: USA
> size: 3"

BYE BYE
Toxic Teddies

SPECS
> produced by: Superfun Company
> origin: USA
> size: 3"

THE KILLER
Toxic Teddies

SPECS
> produced by: Superfun Company
> origin: USA
> size: 3"

THE RAMONES TOXIC TEDDIES
Superfun Company

SPECS
> produced by: Superfun Company
> origin: USA
> size: 4" each

BROCKMANN FIGURES
Groovisions

SPECS
> produced by: Cube Works
> origin: Japan
> size: 3" + 5" each

TIM TSUI

DaTeamBronx

What is your background?

Before I became a figure artist, I was a multi-media producer for several years. Always did design-related work like graphic design, web design, game design, character design, illustrations . . . etc. One day while I was just idling, it suddenly dawned on me, "Hey! Why not try designing a figurine, or better still a team of them?" It happened just like that. I guess that's what creativity is all about.

After a few moments of thought, I started to develop the first DaTeamBronx 12-inch figures and exhibited them at the annual Toycon show in Hong Kong. I was quite surprised with the positive feedback I received. The interest from Japanese and American collectors in particular was totally unexpected. This encouragement plus the support from some of the more well-known figure dealers encouraged me so much that I decided to go into it full time. I am now a full-time toy artist.

After my vinyl figure series was released, they too received very positive feedback. Many famous brands like Royal Elastics and Tower Records invited me to do crossover versions. Colette, too, invited me to exhibit at their shop and to speak at the Toyz conference in Paris. I also took part in the Who's Next fashion week show at the invitation of Artoyz France.

What influences and inspires your art and toy design?

I mostly credit my influences to manga and SFX movies. But during my normal daily life, I also focus on all the tiny things that surround me.

What is it about the new Art Toy design that makes it so appealing?

For design, I think it incorporates everyday elements that surround us, with a fresh outlook. They are closer to real life and real street style. I like to add fashion elements to my toys, bling bling, etc.

Where did DAPE come from?

DAPE is short for Da Ape, which is the name of this new series of vinyl toys. Kong and Penny are the first two characters. When I created them in 2004, I thought that there were too many human-style urban vinyl figures in the market, so I tried to turn it a little bit.

As a background story, DAPE is a graffiti crew that regularly goes bombing at night. One night, their spray cans undergo a chemical reaction. The crew, exposed to the toxic incident, find themselves transformed into apes, their clothes and shoes broken because of the sudden change in their bodies.

Can you comment on the Hong Kong Toycon community and what it was like to be involved?

Toycon was a great event for Hong Kong artists to show their creations and designs to people. It definitely allowed more people to get to know my work and allowed me to meet my supporting fans in smaller groups. The Toycon shows stopped last year, but I'm sure that something will be happening again in the near future. Toycon also inspired many similar events being held all over the world now.

What does the future hold for you?

As an artist I am satisfied just to be able to continue the creative process. Of course, every artist wants his work to be widely known and appreciated. For this a successful artist must be able to bridge the gap between creation and meaning. My aim is to do this by making sure that my present and future creations are evolutionary and capture changes in human desires, behavior, and trends.

You may have noticed that major brand owners are changing their brand promotion and building methods. Brand-building trends are changing due to the influence of the Internet and mobile communications. More and more products are promoted not as a single boring *buy me also* item but are linked to trends reflecting art. In my own small way I hope to be able to contribute to this trend.

← ↑

TOFU HEAD KUBRICKS
[opp left + top]
Devil Robots

SPECS
› produced by: Medicom Toys
› origin: Japan
› size: 3" each

TOFU HEAD VINYL FIGURES
[opp right]
Devil Robots

SPECS
› produced by: Medicom Toys
› origin: Japan
› size: 7" + 5"

↓ ↘

CHERRY + MASH
Headlock Studio

SPECS
> produced by: Headlock Studio
> origin: Japan
> size: 8" each

↓ ↘

TIN-PO: DUKK + SEEB
UNKL Brand

SPECS
> produced by: UNKL Brand
> origin: USA
> size: 2" each

BONE BUNNYS
Frank Kozik

SPECS
› produced by: Medicom Toys
› origin: USA
› size: 8"each

MONSTERISM VOL. 3: GRYNT
Pete Fowler

SPECS
> produced by: Playbeast
> origin: UK
> size: 3"

↖ ↑ ↑ ↗

MONSTERISM VOL. 3: [L-R]
CHEF
BROWNIE
NOMADIC TROUBADOR
DEADWOOD
Pete Fowler

`SPECS`
> produced by: Playbeast
> origin: UK
> size: 3" each

←

MONSTERISM VOL. 3: GREEN
Pete Fowler

`SPECS`
> produced by: Playbeast
> origin: UK
> size: 3"

← →

BROTHERSWORKER: TANK
Brothersfree

SPECS
> produced by: Brothersfree
> origin: Hong Kong
> size: 12"

MONSTER TEENS: RUDY
Charles Burns

SPECS
> produced by:
  Sony Creative
> origin: USA
> size: 3"

→

VOODOO DUNNY
Kid Robot

SPECS
> produced by: Kid Robot
> origin: USA
> size: 8"

↓

MAO DUNNYS
Frank Kozik

SPECS
> produced by: Kid Robot
> origin: USA
> size: 8"

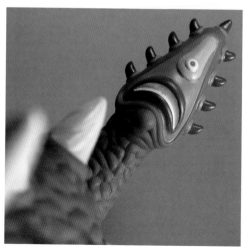

← ↑

DORBEL
Jim Woodring

SPECS
> produced by: STRANGEco
> origin: USA
> size: 7" each

TOYER AND DEVIL TOYER
Toy2R

SPECS
> produced by: Toy2R
> origin: Hong Kong
> size: 8" each

RAYMOND CHOY
Toy2R

How did you start Toy2R?
Did you have a background in
toys prior to beginning?

I started Toy2R in 1995 as a
tiny toy store in Mong Kok
(Hong Kong), selling action
figures from the U.S. and
candy toys from Japan. Prior
to that, I was working as a
quality control manager for a
footwear company, which
required a lot of interactions
with factories in mainland
China. I was a toy collector
for years and became really
interested in the toy industry
while working on a project
making a toy slipper. This
led to me ultimately closing
my retail shop down and
focusing on making my own
toys instead.

Toy2R was one of the regular
participants in the Hong Kong
Toycon community, with a pretty
big presence. Now that Toycon
seems to be finished, what are
your thoughts looking back on
that phenomenon?

Toycon was great for meeting
overseas buyers and promoting our brand products. I
tried to use each Toycon to
introduce as many new toys

as we could and invited our
artists to come meet their
fans. It became an international media event, which
connected us with collectors.
I hope that Hong Kong will
have a toy show like Toycon
again soon!

The Qees are some of the most
successful original designer
toys out there. How did you
develop the idea for the Qees,
and how did you transform it
into a canvas for a wide variety
of artists to customize?

I think Qee has been successful because we were the first
company to open toy cus-
tomization to any designer.
We really pushed the DIY concept way earlier than any
other designer-toy company.
Anyone can download the
design template from our
website, and we are open-
minded about letting artists
play around with the design.

The Qee has sparked a larger
market for the customizable platform toys.

I think the platform toys are
great because they're designed
so people can use them.

How do you choose the artists
that you work with, not only the
core ones like Touma and Jaime
Hayon who develop original toys
with Toy2R but also the artists
who customize the existing toys
like Qees?

If I like their work I will use
them. It's a personal decision.

What are your thoughts on
where the Art Toy market is
going now?

It's definitely slowed down a
lot in Hong Kong; there's not
too much new movement
here. But I can see a lot of
interest from the U.S. and
other countries. I think it's
going strong.

←←
THE GOOD WOOD GANG: [L-R]
BLACKFOOT AKA CAPTAIN BINGO
MR. TTT BURGER
Friends With You

SPECS
> produced by: Friends With You
> origin: USA
> size: 5" + 7"

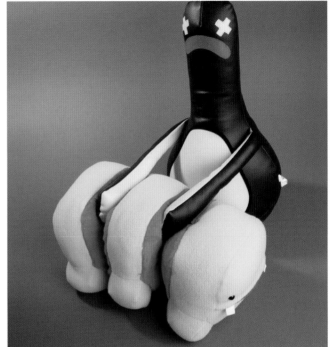

→

MR. TTT + MALFI
Friends With You

SPECS
> produced by: Friends With You
> origin: USA
> size: 20" + 5"

←

THE GOOD WOOD GANG
Friends With You

SPECS
> produced by: Friends With You
> origin: USA
> sizes: various

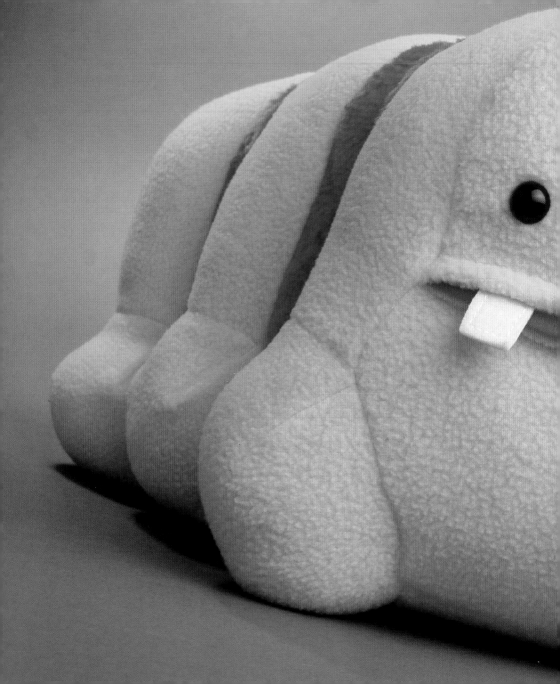

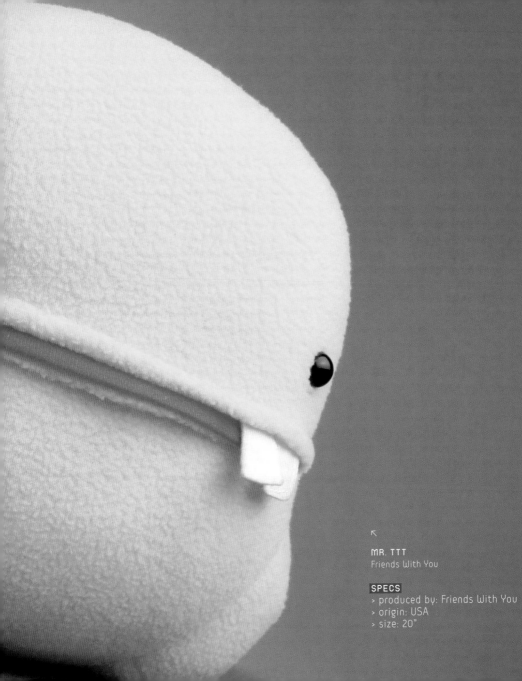

MR. TTT
Friends With You

SPECS
> produced by: Friends With You
> origin: USA
> size: 20"

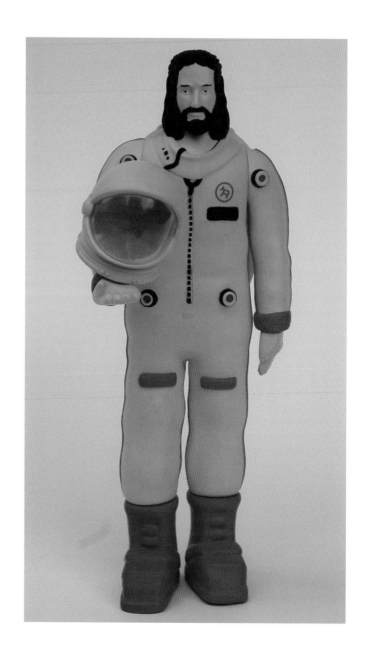

→

ASTRONAUT JESUS
Doma

SPECS
> produced by: Adfunture
> origin: Argentina
> size: 10"

↑

DE LA SOUL
De La Soul

SPECS
> produced by: Thunderbirds
> origin: USA
> size: 7" each

RC-911
Three Zero

THREE ZERO
Three Zero

SPECS
> produced by: Three Zero
> origin: Hong Kong
> size: 7"

SPECS
> produced by: Three Zero
> origin: Hong Kong
> size: 7"

↑
MINI CIRCUS PUNKS [L-R]
TADO, Frank Kozik, NESS,
Lisa Petrucci, Touma

`SPECS`
> produced by: Circus Punks
> origin: USA
> size: 6" each

→
**LIMITED EDITION
CIRCUS PUNKS [opp left]**
Gama-Go, Touma

`SPECS`
> produced by: Circus Punks
> origin: USA
> size: 15" each

→
**LIMITED EDITION
CIRCUS PUNKS [opp right]**
Gary Baseman, Monkey vs. Robot

`SPECS`
> produced by: Circus Punks
> origin: USA
> size: 15" each

NATHAN JUREVICIUS

Scarygirl

What is your background and how did you get involved in making toys?

I've been a full-time freelance illustrator/artist/designer for about ten years working for clients that have included MTV Asia, Comedy Central, Coke, *The Wall Street Journal*, and Warner Bros. A little over three years ago I received a call and email out of the blue from Hong Kong toy company Flying Cat, who asked if I'd like to design toys with them.

Were you a collector before getting involved in the Art Toy movement?

I was a collector of a few things but not Art Toys—this was very new to me when I was first approached.

Who do you cite as your influences, in terms of your art and in terms of your product/toy design?

In terms of art I love Miro, Picasso, Jim Flora, Vitas

Jurevicius (my dad). As far as product and toy design go I'm not really influenced by anyone—just trying to translate what I do in my art into 3D.

What are your ideas/thoughts/realizations on the Art Toy phenomenon?

I like the idea of its crossover aspect—hovering between an art print and sculpture but with the playfulness of an old-school toy. Not sure how long it will remain in the limited-edition/Art Toy side of things for many of the designers.

Has designing toys had an influence on your art?

Maybe in the way I visualize characters a little bit. Subconsciously there's always this thought that possibly I will realize a character as a sculpt and so occasionally think about its form a lot more than I used to.

Typically you see toys being derived from entertainment

properties—merchandising afterthoughts of a larger movie, TV, cartoon, comic, etc. Scarygirl is doing the opposite, going from a product design to an entertainment property with animation and video-game projects. How did that come about, and can you comment on this phenomenon with your work?

I've always tried to create characters with a backstory and personality—this is something very important to me to have the audience engaged in the art and to feel there's something beyond a pretty picture. It also helps motivate me when thinking up ideas. I suppose people have seen this in the work and felt it translates well to other mediums that openly express the backstory (like the film, TV projects, and books). Scarygirl was optioned by Passion Pictures (producers of Gorillaz) over a year ago and currently we are in early development.

↑

CHIHOOHOO + CHIP SPECS
Nathan Jurevicius
> produced by: Flying Cat
> origin: Australia
> size: 6" each

←

SCARYGIRL SPECS
Nathan Jurevicius
> produced by: Flying Cat
> origin: Australia
> size: 6"

↖

BLISTER [opp top] SPECS
Nathan Jurevicius
> produced by: Flying Cat
> origin: Australia
> size: 6.5" each

↙ →

KNUCKLE BEAR
Touma

SPECS
> produced by Toy2R
> origin: Japan
> size: 7"

↗ → →

ONION LOVE INVADER
Jaime Hayon

SPECS
> produced by Toy2R
> origin: Spain
> size: 11"

BROTHERSJOKER: BJ HAMMER
Brothersfree

SPECS
> produced by: Brothersfree
> origin: Hong Kong
> size: 7" each

BROTHERSROBBER
Brothersfree

SPECS
> produced by:
  Brothersfree & Three Zero
> origin: Hong Kong
> size: 12"

DAPE: PENNY
Tim Tsui

SPECS
> produced by: DaTeamBronx
> origin: Hong Kong
> size: 6"

↓

TIM TSUI

ONE DAY WHILE I WAS JUST IDLING, IT SUDDENLY DAWNED ON ME. HEY! WHY NOT TRY DESIGNING A FIGURINE, OR BETTER STILL A TEAM OF THEM? IT HAPPENED JUST LIKE THAT.

↑

IN-CROWD:
YOUNG RUFFIANS +
THE THIN
BLUE LINE
James Jarvis

SPECS
> produced by: Amos Novelties
> origin: UK
> size: 4" each

↓

IN-CROWD:
THE OLD GUARD
James Jarvis

SPECS
> produced by: Amos Novelties
> origin: UK
> size: 4" each

THE AMAZING TWINS
Colan Ho

SPECS
> produced by:
  Another TOYCONcept
> origin: Hong Kong
> size: 6" each

↗

**FIRE WATER
BUNNY: NAKED**
Gary Baseman

SPECS
> produced by: Critterbox
> origin: USA
> size: 2.5"

↗

**FIRE WATER
BUNNY: AQUA**
Gary Baseman

SPECS
> produced by: Critterbox
> origin: USA
> size: 2.5"

↗

**FIRE WATER
BUNNY: BONES**
Gary Baseman

SPECS
> produced by: Critterbox
> origin: USA
> size: 2.5"

↗

**FIRE WATER
BUNNY:
ALL-SEEING**
Gary Baseman

SPECS
> produced by: Critterbox
> origin: USA
> size: 2.5"

← ↖ ↑

DUMB LUCK
Gary Baseman

SPECS
> produced by: Critterbox
> origin: USA
> size: 10" each

↑

HOT CHA CHA
Gary Baseman

SPECS
> produced by: Critterbox
> origin: USA
> size: 7"

↑

THE KINSEY SERIES
Dave Kinsey

SPECS
> produced by: Adfunture Workshop
> origin: USA
> size: 3.5" each

↑

INVISIBLE PLAN
MARS-1

SPECS
> produced by: STRANGEco
> origin: USA
> size: 1.5"-4"

↖

DECO PLAGUE, WRECKER PANDA +
DECO VIRUS QEES [opp top]
Tim Biskup

SPECS
> produced by: Toy2R
> origin: USA
> size: 8" each

←

DECO PLAGUE [opp left]
Tim Biskup

SPECS
> produced by: Toy2R
> origin: USA
> size: 8"

↑

BIRDUZASU + PIGDOG
THE NEO KAIJU PROJECT
Tim Biskup

SPECS
> produced by: STRANGEco/Super7
> origin: USA
> size: 3" each

←

CALLI [opp bot left]
Tim Biskup

SPECS
> produced by: SEG
> origin: USA
> size: 8"

←

GHONNER [opp bot right]
Tim Biskup

SPECS
> produced by: SEG
> origin: USA
> size: 36"

↑

ZLIKS
Andrew Bell

SPECS
> produced by: Wheaty Wheat Studios
> origin: USA
> size: 2"–6"

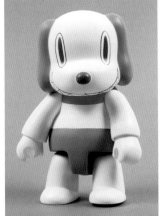

↓

RAYMOND CHOY

ANYONE CAN DOWNLOAD THE DESIGN TEMPLATE FROM OUR WEBSITE. WE ARE OPEN-MINDED ABOUT LETTING ARTISTS PLAY AROUND WITH THE DESIGN.

↑

ONION MON CIRQUE QEE
Jaime Hayon

SPECS
> produced by: Toy2R
> origin: Spain
> size: 2.5"

↑

DOG QEE
Touma

SPECS
> produced by: Toy2R
> origin: Japan
> size: 8"

↑

ONION MON CIRQUE QEE
Jaime Hayon

SPECS
> produced by: Toy2R
> origin: Spain
> size: 2.5"

BOOTED GLAMOUR CAT
Scott Musgrove

SPECS
> produced by: STRANGEco/Wootini
> origin: USA
> size: 5" each

←

TREEBIRD + TRILOMONK
THE NEO KAIJU PROJECT
Kathy Staico-Schorr

SPECS
> produced by: STRANGEco/Super7
> origin: USA
> size: 3" each

→

HUMPTY DJINN + STEAM PUNK
THE NEO KAIJU PROJECT
Todd Schorr

SPECS
> produced by: STRANGEco/Super7
> origin: USA
> size: 3" each

←

TAKO GIRL + NUTHUGGER
THE NEO KAIJU PROJECT
Seonna Hong

SPECS
> produced by: STRANGEco/Super7
> origin: USA
> size: 2.5" each

KEVIN MAK
2da6

2da6 is comprised of myself and my sister Wendy. Our father has been in the toy business since we were kids. To us, toys are not just a business but also our childhood memories. 2da6 is our outlet to focus more on research and concept development.

The whole idea for 2da6 came in the late '90s when the internet was booming hot. We were working with one of the public-transportation companies in Hong Kong. We came up with an idea to use the internet to develop travel packages, in which tourists use the internet to follow clues and ride on the famous Hong Kong double-decker streetcars to explore various cultural areas: fortune-

telling on Temple Street, side street tea houses, etc. The project didn't work out, but we kept the conceptual idea until 2000 when the Government was busy promoting the Small Medium Enterprise (SME) Funding Scheme, which proposed that Hong Kong designers step forward with their own designs. We took the opportunity to re-ignite the idea and put toys and culture together to form the brand 2da6 (pronounced "Yee Da Luk")—meaning an unsung hero or "small potato" who is of no

importance but at times can be portrayed as a local hero who reflects the Hong Kong ethic. 2da6 has evolved from people's language, gestures, and etiquette. All are reproduced in a series of action figures.

Can you comment on the Hong Kong Toycon phenomenon? Where do you see the market going now that Toycon is a thing of the past?

Toycon used to be a hope to any individual who wanted to make his/her dreams come true. It was a platform that starts us off and promotes us/our design to various major markets, such as Japan, the U.S., and a few countries in Europe like France. Without Toycon, Hong Kong toys would be of a different scale and totally different exposure. It is like selling lemonade in our front yard versus in the shopping malls. It sets us up on a higher ground. But after a couple of shows, there were drawbacks to Toycon, and we believe it was the lack of unity and originality. Hong Kong is also known as an instant culture city. Anything can happen overnight. People's tendencies are toward the upbeat, flashy things. They could easily shift from one side to the other, and there is no such thing as an eternity in Hong Kong's materialistic market. Toycon has sadly

faded out, as action figures are no longer a trend. Collectible toys are only for a small number of local collectors or fans. We believe the only way to survive is to shift the design/product from collectibles into mass production.

Gulf and Wayne, your two most prevalent characters, have become spokespeople of a sort for a variety of advertising in Hong Kong. How did this come about, and was this planned from the start?

Nothing in terms of marketing had been previously planned. If it is the case that Gulf and Wayne are the most prevalent characters, the only reason that we can think of is the size of Gulf and the original character of 2da6 for Wayne. Gulf was produced from a unique PVC skin over the skeleton. It was a new 12-inch action figure that most of us hadn't seen in the history of action figures. Our biggest advantage was the price point we set. It turned out to be a good value box set.

How has toy design changed your overall art?

Toys are no longer for children only. Toys are no longer something just to play with. Toys are not just toys . . . they also become a form of expression we can now use.

↗

BUNNYVAN
Jeremy Fish

SPECS
> produced by: STRANGEco/Fifty24SF
> origin: USA
> size: 5"

HELLHOUND
Touma

SPECS
> produced by: Toy2R
> origin: Japan
> size: 6"

↘

KEITH
Spanky

SPECS
> produced by: Headlock Studio
> origin: Japan
> size: 5"

→

CHEECH WIZARD
Vaughn and Mark Bode

SPECS
> produced by: Kid Robot
> origin: USA
> size: 10"

↓

NAAL (TOY PROTOTYPE)
Nathan Jurevicius

SPECS
> produced by: STRANGEco
> origin: Australia
> size: 5" each

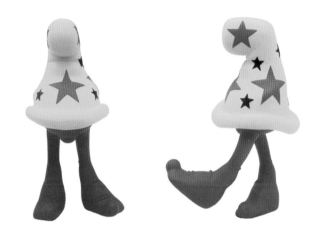

BRUCE LEE AS KATO
Eric So

SPECS
> hand-made custom
> origin: Hong Kong
> size: 12"

ATTABOY

What is your background?

I started out as an illustration student who got seduced by the plastic power of the toy program at FIT in New York City. My roommate at the time was applying and he convinced me to do the same. I'm really not sure how I got in, though, as back then all I really liked to draw was nekkid ladies. I'm sure the 7-foot twinkie sculptures I did at the last minute helped. In high school my two friends Brian and Chris both became heavily involved in toys and animation as well. The immense boredom that far eastern Long Island provided must be held responsible for such tendencies.

What are your ideas, thoughts, realizations about the Art Toy?

It's about freaking time the scales tipped away from the Walmart-opolies and that the lines between art, commerce, sculpture, and character were blurred beyond recognition. See, there are situations which you can't understand or control. And throughout time, whether they were tornadoes, severe draught, or volcanoes, we post-monkey Utopian humans needed to make sense of them, to carry on with each day's up and downs. Aztecs, Romans, Greeks, and Africans, all had created intricate mythologies for explaining why, after working their hardest, they still had a barren harvest and an empty stomach. Even ancient smelly old cave people left character-embodied evidence of fertile-looking women for us to unearth. Statues and icons were figurines of characters they valued and carried to aid them. Characters are the mythology of this modern world and represent our values, good and bad.

In the '50s Reddy Kilowatt, an electric-utility mascot, embodied the assurance that when you flicked a light switch there would be power to preserve your food and light when the sun went down. Today's designer vinyl toys are the closest thing we have to fulfill this inherently human need for unconditional assurance.

What influence has designing toys had on your art?

Heh, you should know better, they're one and the same, mamma. That's why they're called Art Toys, papa. That's what makes this toy revolution so remarkable. Toy design saved my life. Before I went to toy school I thought you had to be completely miserable and pained to create art. I was constantly frustrated, punching walls, never satisfied. Toy design is not just form and function, but concept driven. It's forced me to create worlds in my art where the rules are non-existent and everything is beautifully misspelled, peeled back, and flayed open with its heart a-pumping, like a badly written eighth-grade science report about a dissected frog. Sometimes you can smell the formaldehyde and crayons.

You are a bit unique in that you actually have a background in toy design. Can you speak a little about how this has impacted your understanding of designer-toy culture?

In toy school we could only dream of an environment that fostered what's going on now. Many of us discovered toys from the '60s from Marvin Glass, Ideal, Mego, and Cragstan that share some surprising parallels to the designer toys of today. Back then, companies weren't inundated with teams of reactionary marketing MBA types, but inventors, engineers, and artists. Designer toys are created for many different reasons, and very few are the reasons the majors create their toys, at least currently. Besides my personal characters and approach, I try to infuse actual playability with each of my designer toys, even if it's an interchangeable part—that's very important to me. And that's something I brought from the more mainstream toy world.

How did redesigning classic kids' games for Hasbro (like Cootie, Ants in My Pants, etc.) come about? Were you able to sneak any subversive elements in there for the kiddies?

Just redesigning them was subversive as hell at the time, retooling a classic line based on a just-outta-school kid's designs. I was a long-haired idiot drawing buck teeth and one-big-eyed insects wearing a tie at a company (Milton Bradley) that's as old as Abraham Lincoln. I pitched the idea to the big guy in charge, and he instructed me to redesign the whole line. The people I worked with and my boss were like rock stars to me, fantastic people who didn't roll their eyes when I incessantly threw concepts at them.

Do you still design for the big companies?

Sometimes I'll consult on a project when a company has something it needs my approach on. I've been doing this for ten years now. Nowadays, I divide my time between doing art shows and designer toys, working on my animation properties, and copublishing a magazine that loves toys, art, and sugar. I view my lifestyle as the art form, and I try to never take that for granted. But doing what I love all the time is hard work. The byproduct is an odorless gas that can cause insanity or death if you're not careful. I must keep the windows open wide enough to let fresh air in but never wide enough for me to jump out.

← ↖

CREATURES OF MASS MANIA [opp]
Derrick Hodgson

SPECS
> produced by: Sony Creative
> origin: Canada
> size: 3" each

↑

CARDBOY
Mark James

SPECS
> produced by: Playbeast
> origin: UK
> size: 3"

DUNCES VANIMAL ZOO
Gary Baseman

SPECS
> produced by: Sony Creative
> origin: USA
> size: 3" each

→

ESSENCE
Madtwinz

SPECS
> produced by: Street Legends
> origin: USA
> size: 8.5"

→

VULTURE
Madtwinz

SPECS
> produced by: Street Legends
> origin: USA
> size: 8.5"

↑

IMPERIAL NEWTS
Jim Woodring

SPECS
> produced by: Sony Creative
> origin: USA
> size: 2.5" each

↑

CRAZY NEWTS
Jim Woodring

SPECS
> produced by: Sony Creative
> origin: USA
> size: 2.5" each

KEN JOHO
Headlock Studio

I have had a toy shop in Nagoya, Japan, since 1997. We had wanted to produce toys for years, but there was no manufacturer in Japan willing to produce such a small number of toys. We finally found a factory in 2001, and production was started at once. We had already finished the production of the prototype before finding the factory.

As soon as we heard about Toycon, we wanted to participate. The first time we exhibited was in 2002, and we had a great opportunity to collaborate with several weekly magazines in Hong Kong.

Our design is conscious of mixing the cultures of Japan, the U.S., and Asia. I think that it is understood that the toys that we produce have been influenced by the street culture in Japan and animation from the U.S.

I think that it will be a lot easier for artists and designers to produce toys, and it is a great mode of expression for artists all over the world. For us, we want to keep introducing unique artists and designers in Japan to the rest of the world through our toy production.

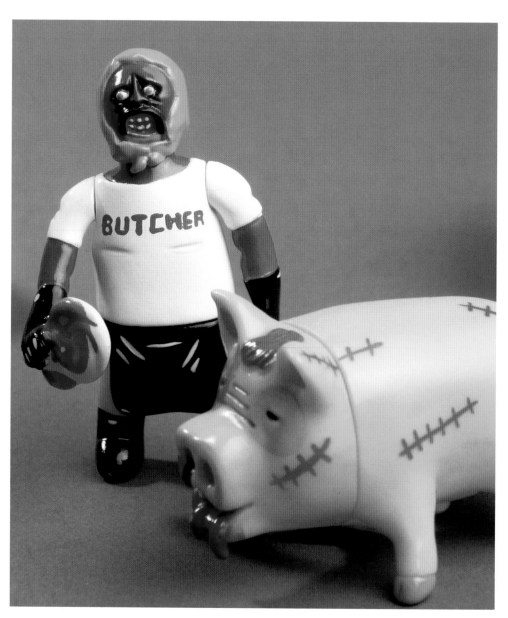

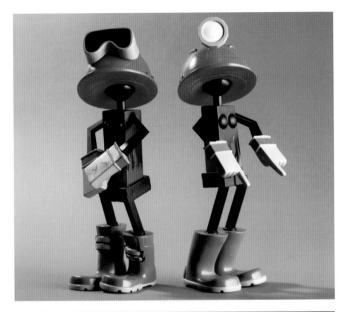

←

AH AUN + AH GUM
Brothersfree

SPECS
> produced by: Brothersfree
> origin: Hong Kong
> size: 8" each

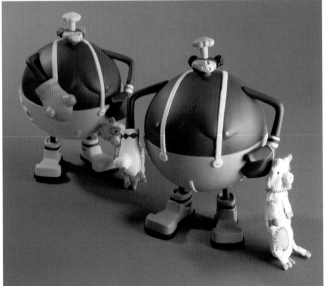

←

BROTHERSJOKER: BJ BOWL
Brothersfree

SPECS
> produced by: Brothersfree
> origin: Hong Kong
> size: 7" each

←

PIGS VANIMAL ZOO
[opp]
Yukinori Dehara

SPECS
> produced by: Sony Creative
> origin: Japan
> size: 2" each

↑ ↗

MONKEY ASSASSIN
Monkey vs. Robot

SPECS
> produced by: Funko
> origin: USA
> size: 6"
> photo: Brian McCarty

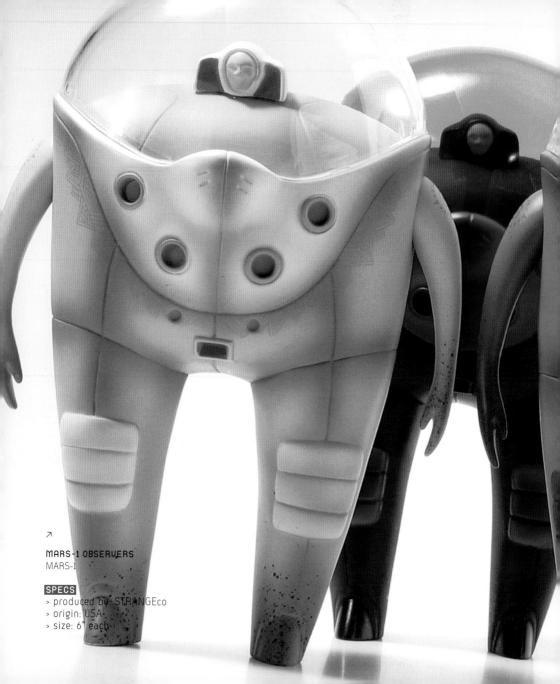

↗

MARS-1 OBSERVERS
MARS-1

SPECS
> produced by STRANGEco
> origin: USA
> size: 6" each

↘

PUSHPAW, PUPSHAW + FRANK
Jim Woodring

`SPECS`
> produced by: Presspop
> origin: USA
> size: 3"-7"

→

LIFE-SIZED PUPSHAW [opp]
Jim Woodring

`SPECS`
> produced by: Presspop
> origin: USA
> size: 14"

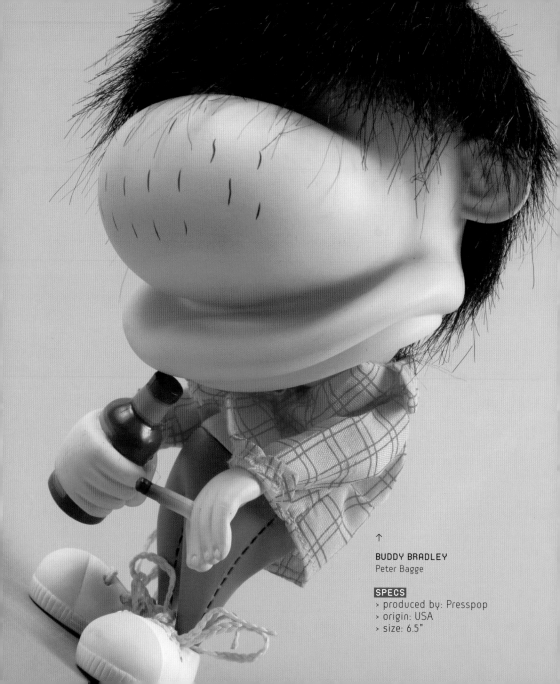

↑
BUDDY BRADLEY
Peter Bagge

SPECS
> produced by: Presspop
> origin: USA
> size: 6.5"

↑

JIMMY CORRIGAN `SPECS`
[top]
Chris Ware
> produced by: Presspop
> origin: USA
> size: 5"

↑

ALIEN FAMILY:
MOM [top] `SPECS`
Peter Bagge
> produced by: Sony Creative
> origin: USA
> size: 2.5"

↑

POGEYBAIT `SPECS`
[bot]
Dan Clowes
> produced by: Presspop
> origin: USA
> size: 5"

↑

**SOF`BOY** [bot] `SPECS`
Archer Prewitt
> produced by: Presspop
> origin: USA
> size: 3"

LEV
Toy Tokyo

I've been working with toys for a long time now. The toys that nobody really considers Art Toys are really where it began for me, though. In the late '80s I was traveling frequently to Asia to get tin wind-ups and robots and other collectibles to sell to my customers back in America. It was hard to ignore the movement happening. My first experience with it was at a toy collectors' meeting in Hong Kong. I bought my first vinyl from Michael Lau himself. After that I was hooked. I began bringing it back to New York, and to the disbelief of many of our customers, it became incredibly popular. A new culture of toy collectors emerged, and it was great. The whole industry got excited again. Now we're involved in production and distribution (as well as our retail and online operations) and working closely with some of the hottest artists.

Toy Tokyo began in 2000 in New York City, but before then I had been selling toys in the Chicago area under a different company name. I have always been fascinated by collectibles from overseas, particularly Japan. At the time I was traveling there extensively to get products, so it makes sense that the store has a little "Japanese flavor." At the same time, though, our store represents toys as well. We cater to collectors from all walks of life and back-grounds. It's a place where you can feel comfortable, whether you are there to grab the latest Godzilla figure or you are trying to find a gift for your little sister's birthday.

We have a reputation for having everything. It's our duty to go beyond the regular toy stores and make sure we get the toys no matter what. We don't just stock what our distributors send us—if there's a hot item that we need to carry, we'll do what it takes to get it. I suppose that could be our philosophy.

Are you a big collector?

Indeed. If you see it in the store or on the website, chances are it's in my private collection. I also collect rare editions, one-of-a-kind items, prototypes, and personalized pieces. Now I have the chance to make sure things get made to go into my collection.

Toy Tokyo has a real "downtown" feel, with The Showroom NYC art gallery across the street and a strong connection with the New York street-art scene.

Being immersed in the culture or "scene" is really the most important part. It keeps you authentic and gives us personality as a company. Having that reputable personality also helps bring everyone together. In our first show we had over 170 graffiti artists, graphic artists, toy designers, and sculptors from all walks of life and fame design one-of-a-kind subway cars for the Tag the System event. The exciting part is when we get to help bring the street culture into the Art Toy/art culture. There is a fascination with street culture right now, and not just in art and Art Toys—you see it all over video games, music, movies, and fashion.

What do you think makes Art Toys so popular?

There are a lot of things that I think contribute to the success of the trend. Of course, there are the fantastic designs that always bring up the demand, but the exclusivity and the affordability of it are also factors. It's also very different from anything we, as toy collectors, have ever seen. It's not an action figure, and it doesn't have kung-fu grip, but it has great

design and they display like fine sculpture. I think it's very exciting to be able to get a designer toy from a world-renowned artist for $60 and know that it's one of only a handful that were produced. Of course, the price point will fluctuate, but that's nothing new to the toy collector.

Where do you see the vinyl toy movement going from here?

As long as the business stays independent I think we are all going to be happy. I see it spreading to different mediums like we're seeing now with all of the plush designs. It's only gotten more and more creative in terms of products, and the exposure is just starting to take effect. We just need to keep quality in mind and make sure to handle it like it's the art it is.

↘

SMOKING CAT
Kaz

`SPECS`
> produced by: Critterbox
> origin: USA
> size: 7"

→

GORILLAZ [opp]
Jamie Hewlitt

`SPECS`
> produced by: Kid Robot
> origin: UK
> size: 7"-13"

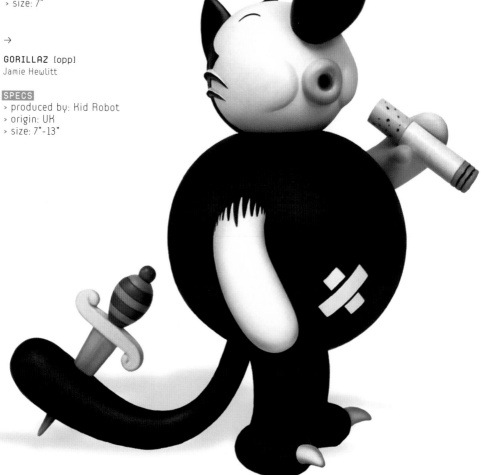

ATTABOY

DOING WHAT I LOVE ALL THE TIME IS HARD WORK. THE BY-PRODUCT IS AN ODORLESS GAS THAT CAN CAUSE INSANITY OR DEATH . . . I MUST KEEP THE WINDOWS OPEN WIDE ENOUGH TO LET FRESH AIR IN BUT NEVER WIDE ENOUGH FOR ME TO JUMP OUT.

→

QWESHUN
Attaboy

SPECS
> hand-made custom
> origin: USA
> size: 5"

←

AKTRYK
Attaboy

SPECS
> produced by: Rock America
> origin: USA
> size: 4.5"

↑

FURILLA
Toren Orzeck

SPECS
> produced by: Furilla
> origin: USA
> size: 12"
> photo: Brian McCarty

 ↑

MULLETHEADS: RANDY LAUGHLIN
Achy Breaky Toys

SPECS
> produced by: Achy Breaky Toys
> origin: USA
> size: 2.5"
> photo: Brian McCarty

→

MICRO + UNDERSON
Headlock Studio

SPECS
> produced by: Headlock Studio
> origin: Japan
> size: 2" + 7"

↓

WONDERFULMAN
Wonderful Designworks

SPECS
> produced by: Headlock Studio
> origin: Japan
> size: 7" each

TALONS + SNOUT
Touma

SPECS
> produced by: Headlock Studio
> origin: Japan
> size: 7" + 5"

140

↖

BUNNYDUCK IN BLACK
Todd Schorr

`SPECS`
> produced by: Necessaries Toy Foundation
> origin: USA
> size: 10"

MIKE "MEZ" MARKOWITZ
Mezco

How did Mezco start and when? Did you have a background in toys or was your interest primarily in collecting?

I started Mezco back in 1999. Mezco owned a company called Aztech Toyz. Aztech shipped a line called Silent Screamers, which was based on old silent monster movies. Aztech came to an end, and I decided that I would forge ahead under the Mezco brand.

The only background I had in toys was my collecting and customizing that I have been doing since I was a wee tyke. I went to the School of Visual Arts in New York City for graphic art, dropped out, was refused acceptance at the FIT toy program, so I said fuck it and started my own company.

Mezco was one of the first U.S.-based companies to create original characters in the Hong Kong-influenced Urban Vinyl style. What made you decide to produce the Hoodz?

I had an idea for a graff writer line a few years before we released Hoodz. It was based around figures that could actually write, but I soon realized that it would have cost me a fortune and I would not make it back so I shelved it. Then when I started seeing what was being done with Urban Vinyl in Hong Kong, I was like, "Oh that's it! It's more of a fashion figure vibe than an action figure that can write graff thing!" I reworked some of the characters that I had stuck in my old sketch book, and then I met with both Michael Lau and Eric So to ask if they would be interested in working with me on this. I felt that I was drawing much from what they had started, and that karmically I didn't feel right not approaching them. Anyway both said no for their own reasons (basically busy doing what they had going on). So I went ahead and tightened up Hoodz, and then I was off to the races. I was impressed with how urban lifestyle had influenced designers in Hong Kong, and my idea was something a bit more focused on graff, kinda like Urban Vinyl complementing urban art.

Mezco seems to mostly create action figures based on entertainment licenses. What do you think of the designer-toy niche, and how does Mezco fit into it?

Regardless if we are working on a licensed project or a homegrown one, it is design driven. My basic philosophy is to make a product that is about lifestyle and design more than a straight-up toy. Of course there are exceptions, but that is the general rule of thumb. I think that the designer-toy niche is also a lifestyle concept more than a toy concept. So on a lot of levels I see strong parallels between Mezco and the designer toys out there. So what do I think of "designer toys"? I love that there has been more art imbedded into toys. We have taken licensed figures and put our own design twist on them (see our Scarface, Blues Brothers, Animal House, and so on for examples of that). As for how we fit in, we all try our best here to make cool shit.

How did the Run-DMC license happen?

While I was working on Hoodz I thought that doing rap figures in a similar fashion would be cool. The only logical group to start with as far as I was concerned was Run-DMC. It all just seemed to make sense and fit together nicely. Graffiti was one of the foundations of what has become urban marketing. It was an underground art movement that has now been utilized worldwide and in high profile. Hip-hop was the musical component of the same movement. Run-DMC is the shit I grew up on and were groundbreakers in the rap world. Like I said, it all seemed to just make sense.

One of your Hoodz characters seems to have become the mascot for a very large soft-drink company. How did that come about?

Well, not exactly one of my Hoodz characters. I was approached by Ogilvy & Mather to design a figure to be used in commercials that they were working on for their client Sprite. They had a bunch of my Hoodz figures and wanted something with the same vibe. I worked out some designs and the one that they settled on is indeed close to my "Letterman" figure from Hoodz. The Sprite project was a straight work-for-hire gig, but it's a blast to see Mr. Thirst pop up on the tube.

↓

MY BASIC PHILOSO-PHY IS TO MAKE A PRODUCT THAT IS ABOUT LIFESTYLE & DESIGN MORE THAN A STRAIGHT-UP TOY.

→

LIVING DEAD DOLLS: (clockwise L-R) **BLUE, TOXIC MOLLY, DAWN, PURDY**
Mezco

SPECS
> produced by: Mezco
> origin: USA
> size: 9" each

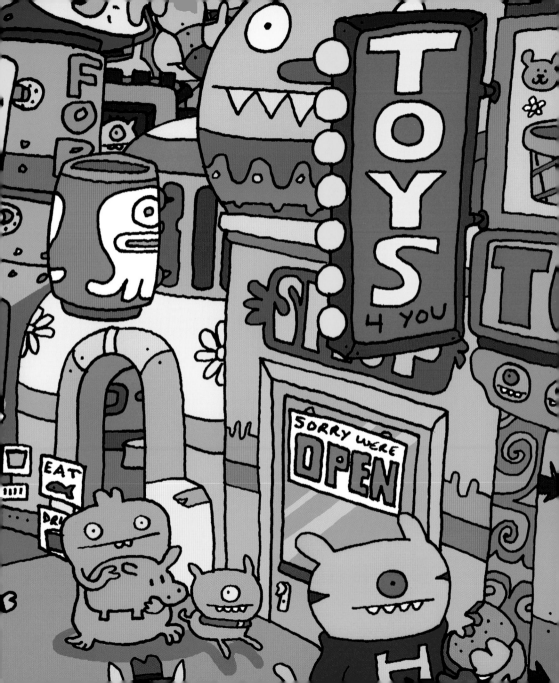

KIM FUNG WONG
Three Zero

Three Zero was one of the originators of the Hong Kong Toycon community. Can you talk about your experience? How did you get involved with Toycon, what was it like to see it grow, etc.?

Actually, I never exhibited at the Hong Kong Toycon, but I was involved in an organization that came before Toycon. I founded my brand Three Zero in 1999, but before that I had a small toy shop called Toon House. In 1996 I founded the Hong Kong Toy Club with two other toy shop owners. The club sponsored a toy expo that appealed directly to collectors (as opposed to the big Hong Kong Toy Fair which was only open for the trade).

The first Toy Club Expo was in 1997, and a lot of members asked if they could put their collections on display. Two of the Toy Club members—Michael Lau and Eric So—also provided some of their original toy designs. That's really what started getting collectors interested in designer toys. The interest convinced the Toy Club committee to change its focus and concentrate exclusively on designer toys.

I was too busy to be a committee member of Toy Club and resigned in 1998.

Did you have a background in toys before starting your company and making your own products?

I was a toy collector and also a toy retailer. Many of my customers were hardcore collectors, and they always complained that the quality of toys didn't meet their expectations. As a collector, I totally understood their feeling. I was thinking maybe I can help them out by producing some high-quality toys. This led me to start planning my own production company.

How did the gas-mask theme (which is used in a lot of your toys) and your logo get designed?

The first toy I produced was a 12-inch figure of a Hong Kong police SDU (Special Duty Unit) officer. It was a real local project, and one of its accessories was a gas mask. Michael Lau was a big collector of 12-inch action figures and really liked the figure. I asked him to help me with the art and design for the brand. Gas masks have three "zeros" (the two eyes and the respirator), so this inspired the logo design and the brand.

Do you have any new Three Zero figures in the works?

Not right now, but I am producing a lot of toys for other companies. Maybe someday, when I find the right project, I will do something new for Three Zero.

Where do you see the worldwide designer vinyl-toy scene going from here?

Designer toys are another style of art and pop culture. Anyone can be an art collector—you don't have to be a millionaire to collect sculpture. Anyone can be a designer, too—you don't have to be Keith Haring or Andy Warhol. Anyone can make toys now, too—you don't have to be Hasbro anymore. Everyone gets what they want!

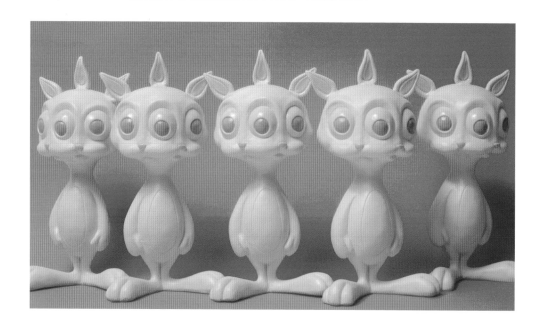

↑

RONNIE RABBBIT
Ron English

SPECS
> produced by: Dark Horse
> origin: USA
> size: 9"

→

McSUPERSIZED
Ron English

SPECS
> produced by: Toy Tokyo
> origin: USA
> size: 8"

MUMMY THE RABBIT
Furi Furi Company

SPECS
> produced by: Furi Furi Co.
> origin: Japan
> size: 7" each

←

BUNNIGURU
Nathan Jurevicius

SPECS
> produced by: Flying Cat
> origin: Australia
> size: 9"

↓

SMORKIN' HATE DUNNYS
Frank Kozik

SPECS
> produced by: Kid Robot
> origin: USA
> size: 3"+ 8"

↑

MASKS 01 + 02
[bot left]
Eric So

`SPECS`
> produced by: Phase 02
> origin: Hong Kong
> size: 6" + 8"

↑

SPRITE VINYL FIGURES
[top]
Eric So

`SPECS`
> produced by: Devilock
> origin: Hong Kong
> size: 7" each

↑

TOYOTA PROMOTIONAL FIGURES
[bot right]
Eric So

`SPECS`
> produced by: Toyota
> origin: Hong Kong
> size: 12" each

↑

GULF [top]
2da6

SPECS
> produced by: 2da6
> origin: Hong Kong
> size: 12"

↑

SPIDER PANG [bot]
2da6

SPECS
> produced by: 2da6
> origin: Hong Kong
> size: 12"

↑

GULF [top]
2da6

SPECS
> produced by: 2da6
> origin: Hong Kong
> size: 12"

↑

SAM "THE BUMMER" [bot]
2da6

SPECS
> produced by: 2da6
> origin: Hong Kong
> size: 12"

↑

WAYNE [top]
2da6

SPECS
> produced by: 2da6
> origin: Hong Kong
> size: 12"

↑

MASTER YAU FUNG SHUI [bot]
2da6

SPECS
> produced by: 2da6
> origin: Hong Kong
> size: 12"

↑

STINKY CLOVE [top]
Shawn Smith

`SPECS`
> produced by: Shawnimals
> origin: USA
> size: 10"

↑

SLIPPERY SPLUG [bot left]
Shawn Smith

`SPECS`
> produced by: Shawnimals
> origin: USA
> size: 10"

↑

WEE NINJA [bot right]
Shawn Smith

`SPECS`
> produced by: Shawnimals
> origin: USA
> size: 7"

LONELY DOLLOP
Shawn Smith

SPECS
> produced by: Shawnimals
> origin: USA
> size: 6"

TIGER BABY
[opp]
Sam Flores

SPECS
> produced by:
  STRANGEco/Fifty24SF
> origin: USA
> size: 7" each

→

TRAVELA
Doze Green

SPECS
> produced by:
  Thunderbirds
> origin: USA
> size: 7"

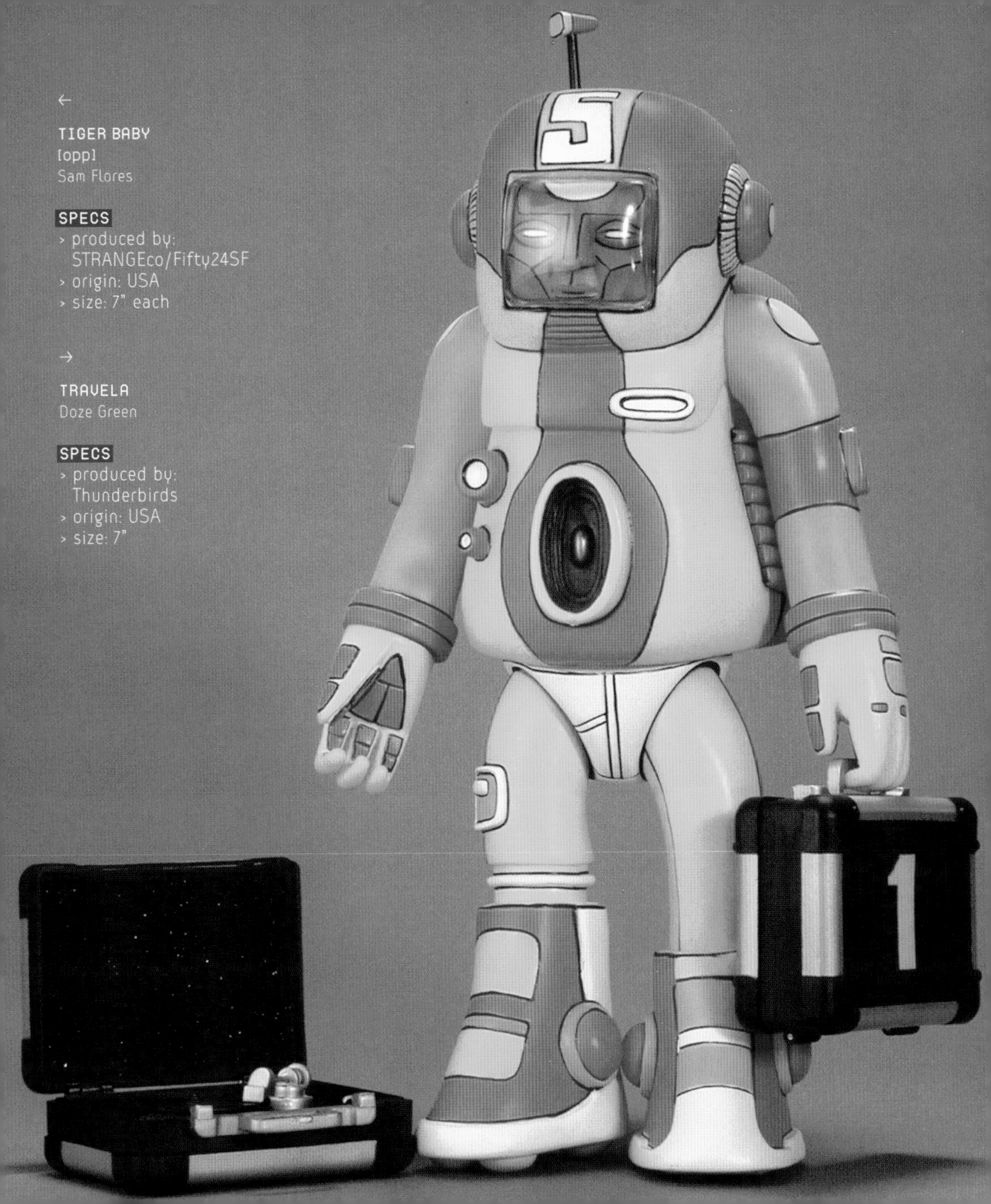

PETE FOWLER

Monsterism

How did you get into designing toys, and what was your art background prior to it?

I got into designing toys through sculpture and wanting to turn my ideas and sketches into physical objects. I had been messing around with clay and plasticine during my fine art degree. I never made the link between toys and my sculptures until much later on and thought of them only as things I made for myself or for fun. I was approached by Sony Creative at a show I had in Japan of my larger sculptures and was given the opportunity to turn them into plastic figures.

Your first toy productions, if I've got it right, were with Cube Works in Japan, which were preceded by some T-shirt designs for the Japanese streetwear label Satan Arbeit. How did all of this come about?

I started to visit Japan through friends and stumbled upon people who were interested in my work and prepared to involve me in their escapades. Satan Arbeit was one of the first breaks for me in Japan, and I was introduced to the boss via a good friend of mine in Osaka. Through working for Satan Arbeit on various clothes-based designs, awareness of my work has grown in Japan and I've been lucky to continue to work there on and off over the years.

Can you explain the world of Monsterism, its creatures, environment, secret location, etc.?

To be precise, "Monsterism Island" exists on our planet Earth but hidden away from the prying eyes of us inhabitants by the geographic and atmospheric conditions that mask it from satellites, boats, and beam ships. The creatures of the island have been introduced via the world of Monsterism figures and novelties, and the inhabitants are incredibly varied in their forms, culture, societies, habitats, and musical tastes. Although the island is a magical, beautiful, spellbinding, and sometimes frightening place, its inhabitants generally have a down-to-earth day-to-day life that exists amongst the mutated, twisted, and monsterized world.

Rumor has it that an animated feature is in the works.

We are currently getting scripts and ideas developed based on a group of characters traveling on Monsterism Island. I can't really tell you more than that, but we have some great people on board to bring it to life. I hope to get something moving this year, whether that's a pilot for a series or a short film, we'll see. Animation has always been an interest for me and seems to be a natural move with the characters and the world growing and developing.

In addition to amazing toy design, you have become well known from the collaborations with the band Super Furry Animals.

I had some work featured in a local free paper in Cardiff and the band saw it and thought they might like me to design some covers for them. I was approached by Creation, their label at the time, and was commissioned to design their second LP cover and the related singles. Apart from a few releases I've been involved with almost all of the visual content of their albums and accompanying stuff. Over the past several years I've worked closely with Mark James both on the design work and on the dartboard.

As one of the most prominent and earliest designers making Art Toys, where do you see the designer vinyl-toy world heading now?

I'm not sure, but I've seen some recent work by several artists and friends that's taking the plastic object in a different direction. I think maybe the figure aspect of it could morph into forms other than strictly figurative. I also like larger-scale pieces, an example being Jim Woodring's Pupshaw figure, which at around 18 inches tall was large enough to have on the floor in your room. I'd like to see some really fresh and different talents emerge with some stories to tell. And new worlds to explore.

GIANT MONSTROOPERS
Pete Fowler

SPECS
> produced by: Playbeast
> origin: UK
> size: 7" each

SUG
UNKL Brand

SPECS
> produced by: UNKL Brand
> origin: USA
> size: 9" each

↑

THE GOOD WOOD GANG
Friends With You

SPECS
> produced by: Friends With You
> origin: USA
> size: 5" each

←

HELPER
Tim Biskup

SPECS
> produced by: Critterbox
> origin: USA
> size: 10"

←

HELMET THE HOT DOG MAN
Will Sweeney

SPECS
> produced by:
  Amos Novelties
> origin: UK
> size: 8"

↓ ↘

THE NEO-KAIJU PROJECT
STRANGEco/Super7

SPECS
> produced by:
  STRANGEco/Super7
> origin: USA
> size: 4" each

TINPO
UNKL Brand

SPECS
> produced by: UNKL Brand
> origin: USA
> size: 2.5"

←

DUNCES
Gary Baseman

SPECS
> produced by: Critterbox
> origin: USA
> size: 8"

↑

BOOTED GLAMOUR CAT
Scott Musgrove

SPECS
> produced by: STRANGEco/Wootini
> origin: USA
> size: 5"

↓

PIP + NORTON
Dave Cooper

SPECS
> produced by: Critterbox
> origin: USA
> size: 5" each

→

MAD*L
Jeremy Madl

SPECS
> produced by:
  Wheaty Wheat Studios
> origin: USA
> size: 5.5"

→

MONSTERISM VOL.3: THE WOODLAND
Pete Fowler

SPECS
> produced by: Playbeast
> origin: USA
> size: 3"

←

ENID
Dan Clowes

`SPECS`
> produced by: Necessaries Toy Foundation
> origin: USA
> size: 12"

↑

KEN'S MYSTERIOUS WORLD
Pete Fowler

`SPECS`
> produced by: Sony Creative
> origin: UK
> size: 2.5" each

↓

`PETE FOWLER`

"MONSTERISM ISLAND" EXISTS ON EARTH BUT IS HIDDEN BY THE GEOGRAPHIC AND ATMOSPHERIC CONDITIONS THAT MASK IT FROM SATELLITES, BOATS, AND BEAM SHIPS.

↓

STEROTYPE II: ARMY OF DEATH
Superdeux

SPECS
> produced by: Red Magic
> origin: France
> size: 2" each

HOODZ:
SIGNSTEIN, VAPORS, FAT CAP
Mezco

SPECS
> produced by: Mezco
> origin: USA
> size: 6"- 7"

←

ELWOOD [opp L]
MOLLY RINGWORM [opp R]
Funko

SPECS
> Spastik Plastik Series
> produced by: Funko
> origin: USA
> size: 5"

↙

T-BONE THE COW [opp bot L]
FUSKA THE CLOWN [opp bot R]
Funko

SPECS
> Spastik Plastik Series
> produced by: Funko
> origin: USA
> size: 5"

↓

SAM THE PIG
Funko

SPECS
> Spastik Plastik Series
> produced by: Funko
> origin: USA
> size: 5"

SEEN

I was born and raised in a quiet residential area of Da' Bronx in New York City. I am a self-taught artist, with no formal training whatsoever—everything I've ever done I learned myself. When I was eleven years old I discovered graffiti and as soon as I saw it, I knew I wanted to be a part of this secret society. Everyone wrote under an alias, mine was "SEEN"—I guess because that's what I wanted to be: seen. I thought it was so great that I could write my name on a train in Da' Bronx and within an hour it would be seen in Brooklyn. Money couldn't buy advertising like that. I've also been obsessed with customizing cars, bikes, and vans, and have been tattooing for years. Although I've been retired for a decade, Tattoo Seen is still going strong.

In the '80s, I was one of a handful of artists that were taken from the streets and introduced to the canvas. At that time the art world was lacking something new and fresh and we were their supposed answer. I was constantly moving until 1988, hopping from one country to another. After a while I felt I was running in circles in the art circus and I needed to step out of the picture to find myself and take a break from the whole "art scene." I kept on creating and experimenting with sculptures and abstract paintings but I kept my distance from the galleries until the mid-'90s. When I came back I found that the crowd had changed; the audience was much younger. It was exciting because over the years my artwork had changed, too. The only problem was that my name was so associated with graffiti that I found myself being pulled backward instead of forward. I was discovering the true meaning of being "labeled," and for this my artwork suffered. I was immediately roped into reliving the past and joining the graffiti crowd again because that's what people expected—but it wasn't what I wanted. Don't get me wrong, I love graffiti and everything it did for me, but I could only do so much. As an artist, I felt I needed to evolve and leave the past in the past—but demand held me back! So I started to turn down exhibitions and began testing my hands in other mediums, including toys.

What was the first toy you produced?

One day about twelve years ago I decided to take one of my characters—the Spraycan Monster—and turn him into a 3-D prototype. When I was finished the first thing I said to myself was, "Wouldn't it be cool to see him as a real toy?"—kind of like a backward Geppetto. He sat around for years until Lev from Toy Tokyo came by my studio with a Japanese toy producer to see my artwork. The first thing they saw was my monster sitting on the filing cabinet. I could hear the excitement in their voices as they asked if they could reproduce him as a limited-edition vinyl figure. Naturally, I said yes. Once I saw the Spraycan Monster complete in the box, I knew for sure that toys were going to be my new adventure.

Has designing toys had an influence on your other art and your exposure to new audiences?

The new toy industry helps show that I'm more than a graffiti artist and that I can design. It's still too early for me to say if it's increased my exposure and notoriety worldwide, but I can't see why not. Not all toy collectors are graffiti fans, so I'm getting my foot in the door right there. I think this new toy phenomenon is a good outlet for artists with a "street art" background like myself because they are in tune with what's going on in the streets. They have a strong relationship with collectors. Being so close in age they share the same interests from music to fashion and art—compared to the corporate giants who really have no clue what's going on today. Most of the "suits and ties" are overdue for retirement. In my opinion the days of baby blocks are on their way out.

How did the Phony-Baloney project get started? Have you found any love from our nation's finest as a result?

Ironically, the Phony-Baloney project was created back in 1987 when my two brothers and I owned the silk screening company called Tuff City Tees. We started printing the Phony-Baloney designs on T-shirts with eight to ten colors and sold them throughout New York. The funniest thing was that most of the people buying the T-shirts were friends and family of police personnel. They were buying them as gag gifts. Last year when I was going through my storage space I came across the old Phony-Baloney designs and said to myself, "It's time to see these guys in 3-D." So we had sculpts made, added a few new characters to update them, and now they're in production. I've been getting a good response from everyone. I think this is due to the fact that many people can relate to them. I think everyone's had at least one bad encounter with law enforcement.

Has designing toys had an influence on your other art and expression?

Somewhere in the future you will be able to see the influence of toy designing in my artwork. I have so many ideas swirling around in my head that I can't wait to sit down and get them out. It's been years since I've created for myself, it's going to be like a breath of fresh air.

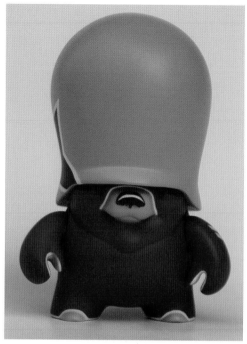

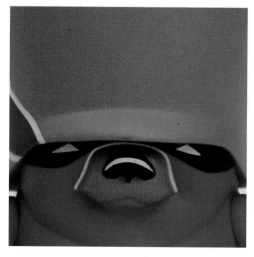

↑ ↗ →

TEDDY TROOPS
Flying Fortress

SPECS
> produced by: Adfunture
> origin: Germany
> size: 3.5" each

HELMUT THE HOT DOG MAN
Will Sweeney

SPECS
> produced by: Amos Novelties
> origin: UK
> size: 8"

ICE-BOTS
Dalek

SPECS
> produced by: Kid Robot
> origin: USA
> size: 2.5" each

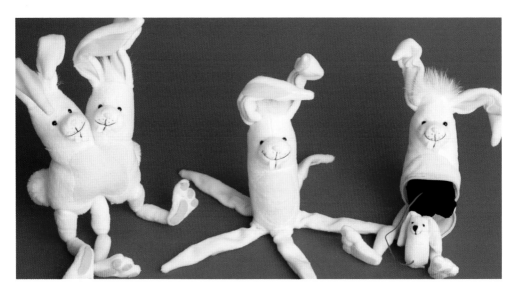

↑

BUNNYWITH PLUSH DOLLS [top]
Alex Pardee

`SPECS`
> produced by: Rock America
> origin: USA
> size: 10" each

↑ →

WORKING PIGS
Furi Furi Company

`SPECS`
> produced by: Sony Creative
> origin: Japan
> size: 2.5" each

↑

THE ROCKET CLUB
Colan Ho

SPECS
> produced by: Another TOYCONcept
> origin: Hong Kong
> size: 3"

↑

MECHABOT
Steve Forde

SPECS
> produced by: Go Hero
> origin: USA
> size: 7"

STEREOTYPE SERIES 1:
BE MY SLAVE
Superdeux

SPECS
> produced by: Red Magic
> origin: France
> size: 2.5" each

CI BOYS
Red Magic

SPECS
> produced by: Red Magic
> origin: Hong Kong
> size: 2.5" each

WE WERE A SMALL CLOTHING COMPANY PRODUCING A TOY AND WE WERE BLOWN AWAY BY OUR ABILITY TO DO THIS. TOYS WERE FOR MASS PRODUCTION!

↓
RUSSELL WATERMAN

→

KING KEN
James Jarvis

SPECS
> produced by: Amos Novelties
> origin: UK
> size: 12" each

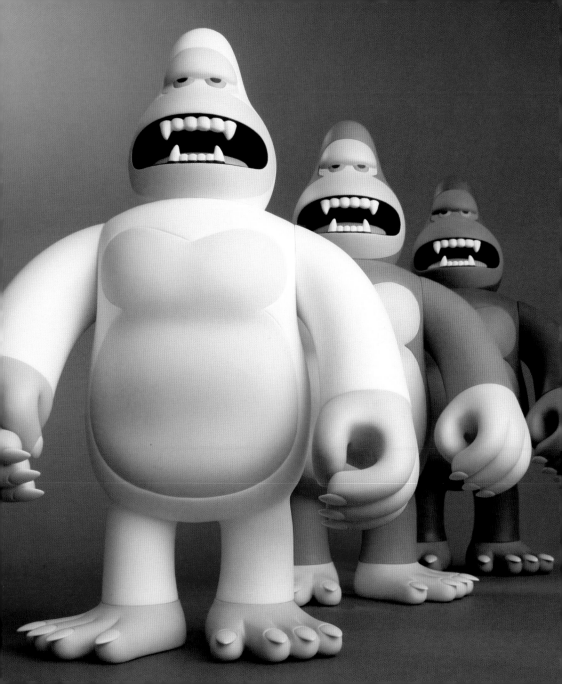

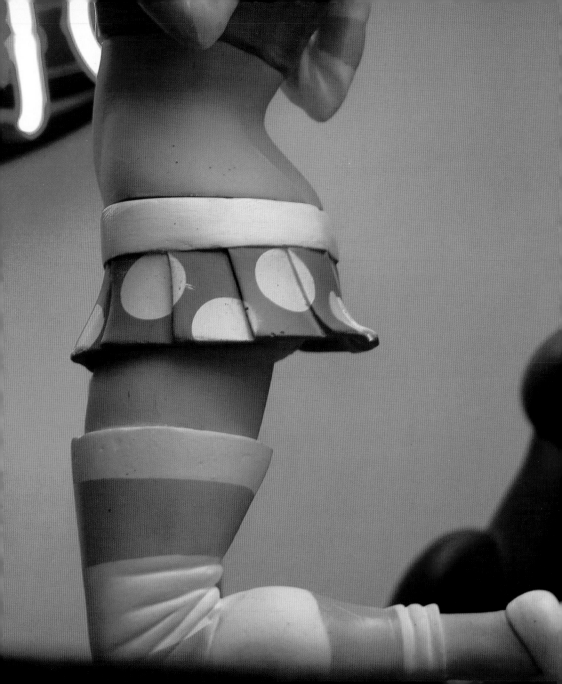

← ↑ ↗

IRINA
Fafi

`SPECS`
> produced by:
  Necessaries Toy Foundation
> origin: France
> size: 10"

↑

FAFI GIRLS
Fafi

`SPECS`
> produced by: Adfunture
> origin: France
> size: 7"

↓

`FAFI`

EVERY REALIZATION IS APPEALING BECAUSE OF ITS ACHIEVEMENT, BUT HOLDING YOUR CREATION IN YOUR HANDS IS UNBELIEVABLE.

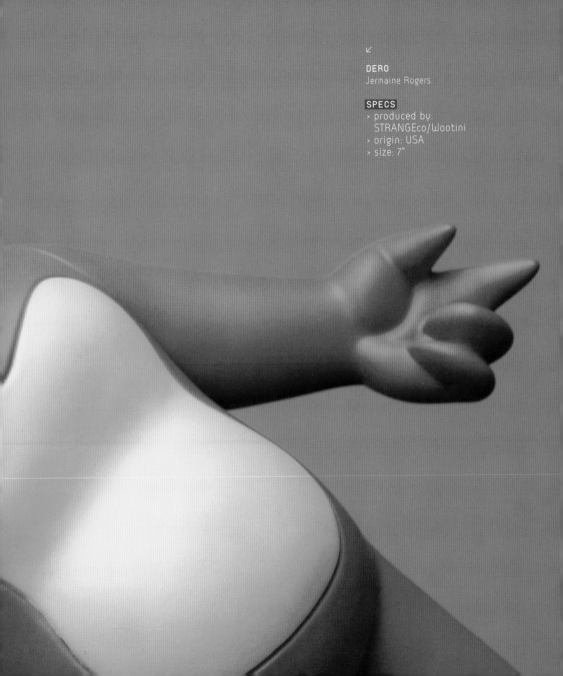

↙

DERO
Jermaine Rogers

SPECS
> produced by:
  STRANGEco/Wootini
> origin: USA
> size: 7"

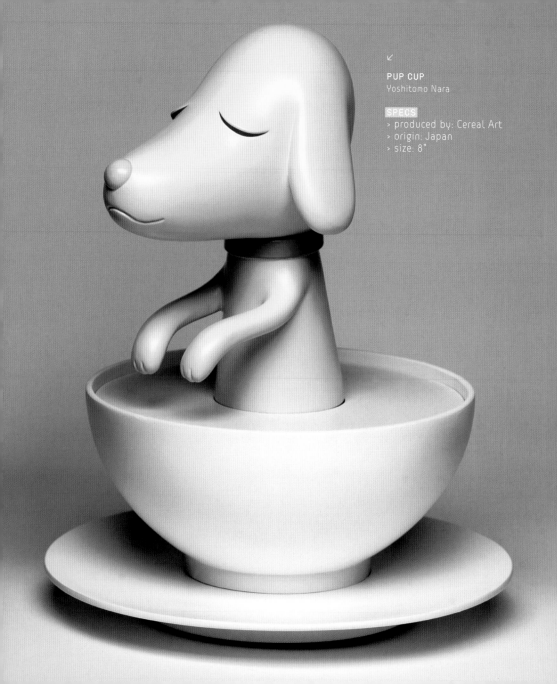

PUP CUP
Yoshitomo Nara

SPECS
> produced by: Cereal Art
> origin: Japan
> size: 8"

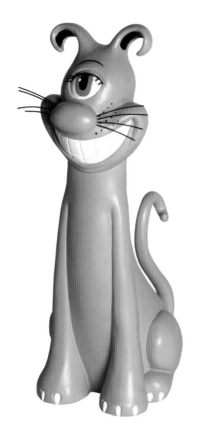

← ↑

CATEYEGUY + DOGEYEGUY
Kenny Scharff

SPECS
> produced by: Cereal Art
> origin: USA
> size: 10"

←

**THE MONSTERS OF
WINNIPEG FOLKLORE**
Marcel Dzama

SPECS
> produced by: Cereal Art
> origin: Canada
> size: 3.5" each

← ↘

KAIJU KIDZ
Ralph Cosentino

SPECS
> produced by: UFO Toys
> origin: USA
> size: 7" + 3"

↑ ↑

EVIROB KUBRICK SERIES 1 + 2
Devil Robots

SPECS
> produced by: Medicom Toys
> origin: Japan
> size: 3" each

↑

STEREOTYPE 3:
FROM OUTER SPACE
Superdeux

SPECS
> produced by: Red Magic
> origin: France
> size: 2" each

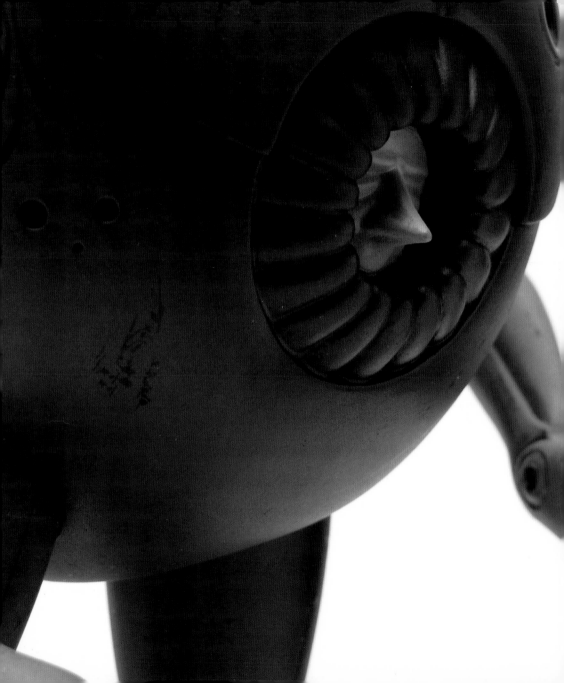

← ↖ ↑ ↑

MARS-1
MARS-1

SPECS
> produced by: STRANGEco/Recon
> origin: USA
> size: 7" each

↑

CACTUS FRIENDS: [L-R] SANDY, BASTARDINO, SABOCHAN
tokidoki

SPECS
> produced by: STRANGEco
> origin: Italy
> size: 2.5"-6"

↑
IN-CROWD WRESTLING FEDERATION
James Jarvis

SPECS
> produced by: Amos Novelties
> origin: UK
> size: 3.5" each

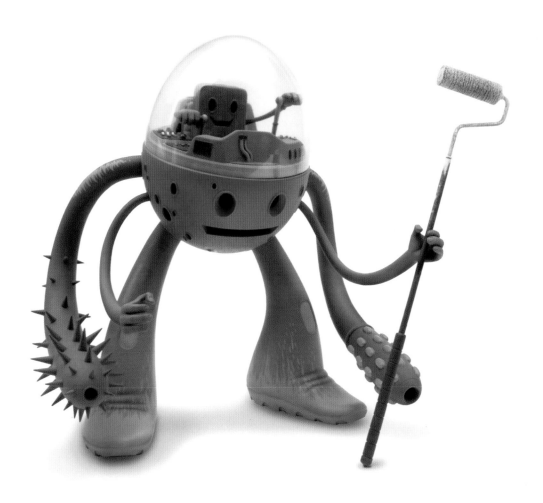

↓
CREDITS & ACKNOWLEDGMENTS

SERIES EDITOR: Jacob Hoye
ART DIRECTION: THE BRM
EDITED BY: Jim Crawford & Gregory Blum
PHOTO EDITOR: Walter Einenkel
PHOTOGRAPHY: Kyle Baker & Gregory Blum
ADDITIONAL PHOTOGRAPHY:
   Brian McCarty/McCarty Photoworks
PROJECT COORDINATOR: Emily Brough
LIVE ACTION INSPIRATION: [L-R] Rei, Juno & Lucas

SPECIAL THANKS TO:
Brin Berliner, Lollion Chong, Hillary Cohen, Augie Corvino, Catherine Crawford, Gaston Dominguez-Letelier, Michael Doret, Maki Hakui, Elizabeth Hill, Wenonah Hoye, Estella Hoye, Elissa Hoye, Liz & Ken Ishii, Izumi Iwasa, Larisa Jacobson, Kathleen Jayes, Keri Jioia, Sung-Fen Kuo, Michelle Lo, Mario Martinez, Charles Miers, Yoshiko Nishiguchi, Jennifer Post, Reuben Rude, Lisa Silfen, Laura Smith, Tiger, Vago, Lisa Waters

ART CREDITS:
PAGE 4: *Space Monkey*, Dalek | PAGE 5: *Mantra*, Jim Woodring | PAGE 6: *Kuku*, Superdeux | PAGE 7: *Heenie*, Nathan Jurevicius | PAGE 8: *Bunnyvan*, Jeremy Fish | PAGE 9: *King Ken*, James Jarvis | PAGES 24-25: *Friends With You*, Friends With You | PAGE 60 (bot right): *Friends Vessel*, Friends With You | PAGE 72 (bot left & right): *On the Run* and *Cyclops*, Nathan Jurevicius | PAGE 93: *An Alien in the Land of Make-Believe*, Todd Schorr | PAGES 94-95: *Antoinette, the Sympathy Girl*, Nathan Cabrera and Pablo, photo by Brian McCarty | PAGES 108-109: *Dunces*, Gary Baseman | PAGE 130-131: *Space Monkeys*, Dalek | PAGE 140: *Irina*, Fafi | PAGE 141: *Gefilte*, Gary Baseman | PAGE 143: *Romantic Notions of the Mysterious East*, Todd Schorr | PAGES 148-149: *Uglytown*, David Horvath | Pages 204-205: *Prob-u-lem*, Jim Woodring | PAGE 210: *Tribes of Monsterism*, Pete Fowler | PAGE 211: *IMAC Zombies*, LMAC | PAGE 212: *Firecat*, Joe Ledbetter | PAGE 213: *Naal*, Nathan Jurevicius | PAGE 214: *Original Toy Monkey*, Gary Taxali | PAGE 215: *Walker*, Jeff Soto

STRANGEco is the foremost purveyor of artist-designed action figures and toys. Founded in 2002 by Gregory Blum and Jim Crawford, STRANGEco has been instrumental in popularizing international Designer Toy culture by creating, distributing, and promoting Art Toys in the U.S. and abroad. STRANGEco won't stop until every freedom-loving comrade has a designer toy on his or her shelf, computer, kitchen counter or hi-fi console. Visit STRANGEco online at www.strangeco.com.